MOUNT CLEMENS PUBLIC LIBRARY
150 Cass Avenue
Mount Clemens, MI 48043
(586) 469-6200

8/07
DEMCO

WORLD IN FOCUS

FOCUS ON
Turkey

ANITA GANERI

WORLD ALMANAC® LIBRARY

Please visit our web site at: www.garethstevens.com
For a free color catalog describing World Almanac® Library's list of high-quality books
and multimedia programs, call 1-800-848-2928 (USA) or 1-800-387-3178 (Canada).

Library of Congress Cataloging-in-Publication Data available upon request from publisher.

ISBN 978-0-8368-6753-4 (lib. bdg.)
ISBN 978-0-8368-6760-2 (softcover)

This North American edition first published in 2008 by
World Almanac® Library
A Weekly Reader Corporation imprint
200 First Stamford Place
Stamford, CT 06912 USA

Commissioning editor: Victoria Brooker
Editor: Nicola Barber
Inside design: Chris Halls, www.mindseyedesign.co.uk
Cover design: Hodder Wayland
Series concept and project management by EASI-Educational Resourcing
(info@easi-er.co.uk)
Statistical research: Anna Bowden
Maps and graphs: Martin Darlison, Encompass Graphics

World Almanac® Library editor: Alan Wachtel
World Almanac® Library cover design: Scott M. Krall

Picture acknowledgments. The author and publisher would like to thank the following for allowing their pictures to be reproduced
in this publication:
CORBIS 8 (Yann Arthus-Bertrand), 13 (Bettmann), 17, 23, 24, 25, 35, 36 (Reuters), 22, 58 (Umit Bektas/Reuters),
34, 59 (Vincent Kessler/Reuters), 56 (Murat Taner/zefa), 57 (Robert Landau). EASI-Images 37 (Miguel Hunt). Ed Parker/Images
Everything/EASI-Images *title page* 4, 5, 6, 9, 10, 11, 12, 14, 15, 16, 18, 19, 20, 21, 26, 27, 28, 29, 30, 31, 32, 33, 38, 39, 40, 41, 42, 43, 44,
45, 46, 47, 48, 49, 50, 51, 52, 53, 54, 55.

The directional arrow portrayed on the map on page 7 provides only an approximation of north.
The data used to produce the graphics and data panels in this title were the latest available at the time of production.

Printed in China

1 2 3 4 5 6 7 8 9 10 09 08 07

CONTENTS

Cover: Modern skyscrapers dominate the skyline of this part of Istanbul, Turkey's largest city.

Title page: The interior of the Hagia Sophia in Istanbul, which was once a Christian church, then a mosque.

CHAPTER 1

Turkey – An Overview

Turkey lies at the crossroads of Europe and Asia, a unique geographical location that has shaped both its history and culture. Since ancient times, Turkey has been a center of civilization, trade and travel. In 1923, the Turkish parliament formally declared the country a republic, and Mustafa Kemal, later known as Atatürk (meaning "father of the Turks"), who had led the Turks to victory in the War of Independence, was elected president.

GEOGRAPHY

Much of Turkey covers a large, mountainous peninsula called Anatolia (Asia Minor), which borders Syria and Iraq to the south, and Iran, Azerbaijan, Armenia, and Georgia to the east. A small part of the country is made up of Thrace, which is part of Europe, and which borders Greece and Bulgaria. Turkey has 4,474 miles (7,200 kilometers) of coastline extending along the Mediterranean, Aegean, Marmara, and Black seas. The country has several large cities including Istanbul, Ankara (the capital), Izmir, Bursa, Adana, Gaziantep, and Konya, as well as areas of rich farmland, but much of the country is high plateau or mountains. The east and southeast are less developed, and, therefore, poorer, than the more densely populated western and southern regions.

A SECULAR REPUBLIC

Turks started to migrate into Anatolia in the 11th century, bringing with them the religion of Islam, which came to replace Christianity as the dominant religion in the region. One group—the Ottoman Turks—emerged as a major force in the 14th century. The Ottomans crossed into Europe in 1360 and made Edirne their capital. In 1453, their leader Sultan Mehmet II

◄ A woman rakes hazelnuts as they dry in the sun near Trabzon, located on Turkey's Black Sea coast. Turkey produces about 75 percent of the world's supply of hazelnuts.

▲ Modern skyscrapers dominate the skyline of this part of Istanbul, Turkey's biggest city.

conquered Constantinople, which became the center of the Ottoman Empire. At its height in the 16th century, this empire governed most of southeast Europe, the Middle East, and North Africa. The empire lasted until after the end of World War I, in the aftermath of which the Turkish Republic was born. The architect of the new republic was Mustafa Kemal, who introduced political and cultural changes in order to modernize Turkey. Kemal created a secular country, outlawing some traditional Islamic practices. In spite of the fact that more than 97 percent of today's population is Muslim, the Turkish Republic has remained a secular state ever since. However, there is ongoing debate in the country between defenders of secularism and those who wish to make Turkey into a more actively Islamic country.

MODERN TURKEY

Turkey is a rapidly developing country that has become industrialized since the 1950s. It has ample mineral reserves and is an important gateway for the flow of commodities such as oil between Europe and Asia. In spite of this, there are huge differences between lifestyles in the wealthy areas of Turkey's west and southwest and the poorer regions of the country's east and southeast. Turkey's government is investing in a huge project in the southeast in order to try to bring more work and prosperity to this region. Turkey is also engaged in ongoing negotiations to become a member of the European Union, or EU.

BEAUTIFUL TURKEY

Turkey is a land of great contrasts, from the wild, rugged mountains of the northern coast to the expanses of the Anatolian plateau, and the dramatic scenery of the Aegean coastline. It is also home to some of the world's most famous archaeological sites, including Ephesus and Troy. Each year, millions of tourists come to the country to enjoy all that Turkey has to offer—fantastic beaches, historical sites, stunning scenery and wildlife, and fascinating cities. Istanbul is a particular attraction, with its long history as the capital of the Roman, Byzantine, and Ottoman empires.

Physical Geography

- Land area: 297,513 sq miles/770,760 sq km
- Water area: 3,791 sq miles/9,820 sq km
- Total area: 301,304 sq miles/780,580 sq km
- World rank (by area): 37
- Land boundaries: 1,645 miles/2,648 km
- Border countries: Armenia, Azerbaijan, Bulgaria, Georgia, Greece, Iran, Iraq, Syria
- Coastline: 4,474 miles/7,200 km
- Highest point: Mount Ararat (16,950 ft/ 5,166 m)
- Lowest point: Mediterranean Sea (0 ft/0 m)

Source: CIA World Factbook

 Did You Know?

Istanbul has had many name changes. It started life as Byzantium. When Emperor Constantine made it the capital of the Roman Empire, it was officially renamed Nova Roma, or New Rome, but it soon became known as Constantinople in his honor. After the Ottoman conquest, it was called Istanbul, although no one knows where this name came from or quite when it was first used.

▼ The Library of Celsus at Ephesus, on Turkey's Aegean coast, is one of the many attractions that brings tourists to this region.

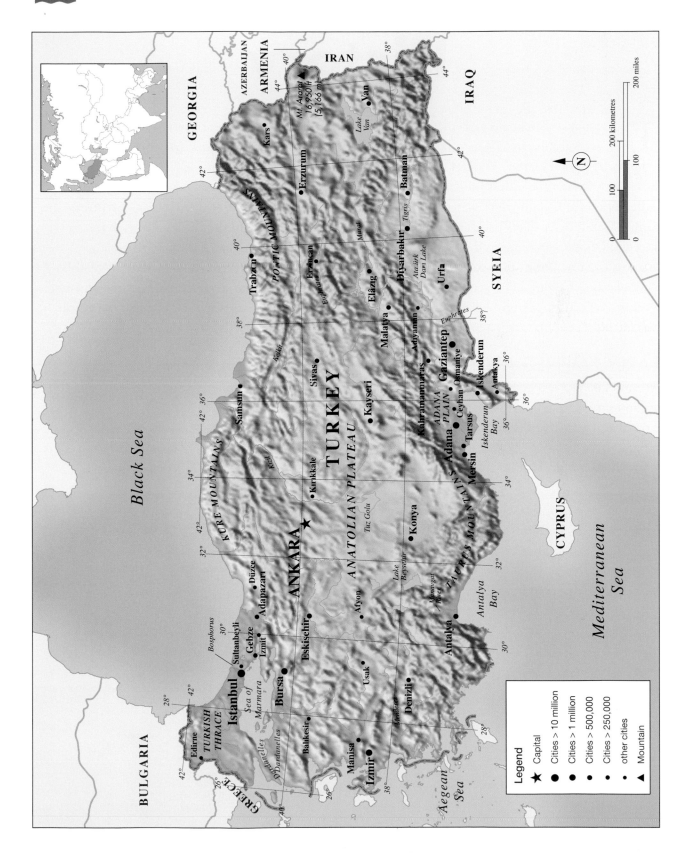

Legend
★ Capital
● Cities > 10 million
● Cities > 1 million
• Cities > 500,000
• Cities > 250,000
· other cities
▲ Mountain

CHAPTER 2

History

The history of Turkey is extremely ancient. The region known as Anatolia was home to nomadic hunter-gatherers from as early as 20,000 B.C. One of the oldest known urban settlements is at Çatalhöyük, near present-day Konya. Çatalhöyük dates back to about 6000 B.C., and from excavations at the site we know that it was a town of mud-brick houses, with a population of about 5,000 people. Metalworking—first copper, and later bronze—was introduced to the region around 5000 B.C.

EARLY EMPIRES AND STATES

Around 2000 B.C., a people called the Hittites began to migrate from central Asia into Anatolia. They established an empire, with its capital at Hattusas (northeast of Ankara), that made them a powerful force in the Middle East.

They developed their own cuneiform writing and knew how to work iron. Their empire flourished until about 1200 B.C., after which areas of Anatolia were taken over by various peoples including the Assyrians, the Phrygians, the Lydians, and the Ionian Greeks. In 546 B.C., the Persians, under their leader Cyrus the Great, conquered part of Anatolia, but the Persians were themselves overthrown by the Greek armies of Alexander the Great in 334 B.C. After Alexander's death in 323 B.C., Anatolia fragmented into a number of independent states which all eventually became part of the expanding Roman Empire.

▼ An aerial view of excavations at the site of Çatalhöyük, near Konya. Finds from this site are displayed in museums in Konya and Ankara.

▲ This relief carving from a museum in Ankara shows a Hittite war chariot.

THE ROMAN EMPIRE

Anatolia became part of the Roman Empire in 133 B.C. During the reign of Emperor Diocletian (A.D. 284–305), the huge Roman Empire was split into eastern and western parts.

The empire was reunited as one under Emperor Constantine who, in 330, created a new imperial capital in the ancient city of Byzantium known as Constantinople (present-day Istanbul), on the Bosphorus Strait. The Roman Empire was divided again in 395, but the western part was soon overrun by invaders. The eastern half, however, became the Byzantine Empire, which lasted until 1453.

Focus on: St. Paul

Born in about A.D. 1 in Tarsus, a town in the south of Anatolia, St. Paul was a Jew who converted to Christianity after experiencing a vision of Jesus on a journey to Damascus, Syria, in about A.D. 36. He preached his first Christian sermon at Antioch (modern-day Antakya) and made three famous missionary journeys around Anatolia and Greece, converting people to Christianity as he went. He was persecuted and eventually put to death by the Romans in A.D. 67. Christians continued to be persecuted in the Roman Empire until Emperor Constantine issued the Edict of Milan in 313, granting them freedom of worship.

◀ Today, the interior of this caravanserai in Kayseri is used to sell rugs. Kayseri, in central Turkey, stood at the meeting point of several trading routes, and it flourished under Roman and Seljuk rule.

THE TURKS

The Turks were originally nomadic, tribal peoples who lived in central Asia. In about the seventh century, some of these nomads began to migrate westward, and during the tenth century many of them converted to Islam. In 1055, one group of Turks, the Seljuk Turks, occupied Baghdad, which was at that time the capital of the Islamic world, and established control over a large empire. In 1071, the Seljuk Turks defeated a Byzantine army at the Battle of Manzikert (in eastern Anatolia) and extended their territory across much of Anatolia. They brought with them the Turkish language, which gradually replaced Greek, and their religion—Islam—which began to replace Christianity. Various states were established in Anatolia, the best-known being the Seljuk Sultanate of Rum (1077–1308) which was based around its capital at Konya.

THE CRUSADES

The empire of the Seljuk Turks extended into Syria and Palestine, a region known as the Holy Land to Christians because it was where Jesus had lived and died. The advance of the Seljuk Turks across the Byzantine Empire and further south into the Holy Land prompted the Crusades, a series of wars from the 11th to the 13th centuries. The First Crusade started in 1096 at Constantinople. The Christian armies crossed Anatolia to capture Antioch (Antakya) in 1098, re-establishing Byzantine control across part of the region as they went. However, in the 12th century, the Seljuk sultans inflicted defeats on the Christian armies, and in the following century the Seljuk Sultanate enjoyed its greatest period both politically and culturally. Seljuk monuments, mostly mosques and caravanserais, can be seen in Konya and elsewhere in Anatolia today. Seljuk rule was interrupted by Asian nomads called the Mongols who invaded Anatolia and defeated the Seljuks in 1243. The last Seljuk sultan died in 1308, but by then the growing influence of another group of Turks—the Ottomans—had begun to be felt.

THE OTTOMAN EMPIRE

The Ottoman dynasty was founded by Osman I in the early 1300s. The Ottomans quickly extended their territories and power and, in 1453, they captured Constantinople, bringing the Byzantine Empire to an end. The Ottomans made Constantinople, which they started to call Istanbul, their capital. Under their greatest ruler, Süleyman the Magnificent (who ruled 1520–1566), the Ottoman Empire covered land from North Africa, in the west, to Iraq, in the east, and northward as far as Hungary. As well as being a skilled military commander, Süleyman was a great patron of the arts and architecture, both of which flourished during his long rule.

After the death of Süleyman the Magnificent, the empire began a gradual decline. In 1571, the Ottoman navy was defeated at the Battle of Lepanto by Spanish and Portuguese forces, and, in 1683, Ottoman troops were forced to withdraw after an unsuccessful siege of Vienna. Loss of power and territory continued throughout the 18th century. For example, after a series of wars against Russia, the Ottomans were forced to allow Russian ships to have access to their waterways and ports under the terms of the Treaty of Kuchuk Kainarji (1774). In the nineteenth century, European countries took over a number of territories that had been part of the Ottoman Empire, and Greece and Serbia became independent, an example followed later by Albania, Bulgaria, and Romania. During World War I, the Ottomans fought with the Central Powers (Germany and Austria-Hungary) against the Allies (Britain, France, and Russia). In 1918, the war ended with the defeat of the Central Powers.

▶ Tourists admire the ornate decoration of rooms inside the Topkapi Palace in Istanbul. The palace was home to generations of Ottoman rulers.

THE END OF EMPIRE

At the end of the war, Istanbul was occupied by Allied troops, and, in 1919, Greek forces under Allied protection landed at Izmir and advanced inland with the intention of seizing territory. Turkish resistance was organized by Mustafa Kemal, an army general who had played a large part in the Ottoman defeat of the Allies at Gallipoli in 1915. Kemal and his nationalist forces drove the Greeks out of Turkey in 1922, and the Allies formed a new peace treaty with the nationalists. In 1923, the Treaty of Lausanne established the new borders of Turkey. The Turkish parliament approved Kemal's decision to abolish the Ottoman Empire. The Republic of Turkey was proclaimed on October 29, 1923, and Ankara was made its capital.

REFORMS

Kemal became the first president of the republic. Beginning in 1925, he introduced sweeping reforms to turn Turkey into a modern, secular state. He abolished religious courts and religious instruction in schools, adopted the Western calendar, encouraged the wearing of Western dress, and banned the *fez*, the traditional Ottoman flat-topped hat. Surnames were introduced, the Roman alphabet replaced Arabic script, women were given the right to vote (in 1930) and to hold public office, and the education system was completely overhauled. Kemal remained as president until his death in 1938. His successor was Ismet Inönü, a leading general of the War of Independence fought against Greece.

CYPRUS

During World War II, Turkey remained neutral, although it declared war on Germany in 1945 in order to take part in the Conference on International Organizations in San Francisco, during which it became one of the founding members of the United Nations. Turkey also joined NATO in 1952, but it had various disputes with its fellow NATO-member, Greece. During the 1960s, Turkey and Greece nearly went to war over Cyprus where there was a Turkish Cypriot minority and a Greek

 Did You Know?

Mustafa Kemal was given the surname Atatürk—meaning "father of the Turks"—by the Turkish Grand National Assembly in 1934.

◀ This memorial in Ankara commemorates the War of Independence fought from 1919 to 1922 by the Turkish nationalist forces. It shows Mustafa Kemal seated on a horse.

▶ Turkish Cypriot refugees shelter in a tent village just outside Nicosia, the capital of Cyprus, after fighting broke out between Turkish and Greek Cypriots in 1964.

Cypriot majority. In 1974, Turkish troops landed on the island in response to the Greek overthrow of the Cypriot president. The result was the partition of the island into the Greek south (two-thirds of the territory) called the Republic of Cyprus and the northern one-third occupied by Turkey, which the Turks call the Turkish Republic of Northern Cyprus (KKTC).

MILITARY AND CIVILIAN GOVERNMENTS

In Turkey itself, the Turkish army has made three interventions in the political process. In 1960, the army staged a coup to prevent the government of the time from, as they saw it, reversing Atatürk's reforms. In 1971, armed forces intervened a second time, and, in 1980, they took over after several years of serious fighting between left- and right-wing extremists. Turkey's armed forces regard

themselves as protectors of Atatürk's principles and legacy, and of secularism. The late 1970s, in particular, were a time of turmoil in Turkey, and, after the 1980 coup, the military moved quickly to restore law and order. Turkey's international reputation, however, suffered as many people voiced concerns over human- rights abuses during this time. Turkey returned to civilian government in 1983.

Some major issues that have dominated politics in Turkey since the 1980s include the rise of the Kurdish nationalist movement and Turkey's proposed membership in the European Union (EU). In 2003, Turkey played a central role in the run-up to the invasion of Iraq. The country refused to allow the United States military to cross its territory, although it did allow U.S. military planes to use its airspace.

Landscape and Climate

Turkey covers 301,304 square miles (780,580 square kilometers), including 3,791 sq miles (9,820 sq km) of water. About 3 percent of the country lies in Thrace, a region of southeastern Europe; the rest is made up of Anatolia, a mountainous peninsula that is part of Asia. The European and Asian parts of Turkey are divided by the Sea of Marmara and two narrow straits—the Dardanelles and the Bosphorus.

SEAS AND LAKES

Turkey is surrounded by sea on three sides. The Black Sea lies to the north, the Aegean Sea to the west, and the Mediterranean Sea to the south. Between the Black and Aegean seas lies the Sea of Marmara, an enclosed sea that is connected to the Black Sea by the Bosphorus Strait and to the Aegean by another narrow sea strait called the Dardanelles. Both the Bosphorus and the Dardanelles are important international trade routes because they link the Black Sea to the rest of the world. Turkey also has a large number of lakes, the biggest being Lake Van in the east of the country (1,433 sq miles/3,713 sq km).

TURKEY'S GEOGRAPHICAL REGIONS

Many people think of Turkey as having seven major geographical regions. The Black Sea

▼ A view across the Bosphorus Strait from the European side of Turkey toward the Asian side.

region is a wild and mountainous area along the country's north coast. High mountain ranges run parallel to the coast, making access to the Black Sea difficult except through a few narrow valleys. Many of the mountain slopes are heavily wooded. In a few places, for example around Samsun and Trabzon, the narrow coastal strip widens into a fertile plain. The Marmara and Aegean regions have extensive fertile plains which are important areas for agriculture. The Marmara region is one of the most densely populated areas in Turkey. In the south of Anatolia, the Mediterranean region has coastal plains that are separated from the rest of Anatolia by the peaks of the Taurus Mountains. The coastal plains are intensively farmed, with cotton as a major crop.

The Central Anatolian region covers the middle of Turkey, and consists mainly of high plateau land where animals are grazed. Further east is the Eastern Anatolian region that is the

▲ The fertile plains near Antalya, on Turkey's Mediterranean coast, are irrigated to raise crops such as corn, pomegranates, and oranges.

largest of the country's geographical regions. It is a land of high mountains, including Turkey's highest peak, Mount Ararat (16,950 feet/5,166 meters), and vast plateaus. Lake Van is situated in these mountain ranges at an altitude of 5,072 feet (1,546 m). It is a very sparsely populated, rugged region, where farming is difficult because of the long, harsh winters and steep mountain slopes. Turkey's seventh region, in its southeast, lies south of these mountains. It is a vast area of rolling hills and plateaus, and, in the far southeast, high mountains.

 Did You Know?

There are many extinct volcanoes in Turkey's mountainous eastern Anatolian region.

winters and hot, dry summers. The Black Sea coast has a lot of rain all year round, with mild winters. The mountains, however, prevent the mild, maritime influence from extending inland. Central and eastern Anatolia have a continental climate with hot, dry summers and very cold winters with heavy snowfalls. Temperatures average over 86° Fahrenheit (30° Celsius) in the summer with little rainfall, while winter temperatures can fall as low as -22° F to -40° F (-30° C to -40° C).

EARTHQUAKES

Geologically, Turkey lies on the Anatolian Plate, a minor tectonic plate that is being squeezed between three major plates—the Eurasian Plate, to the north, and the African and Arabian plates, to the south. The boundary where these plates meet is called the North Anatolian fault, and it extends from east of Erzincan to Izmit, through the Sea of Marmara and into the northeastern Aegean. As a result of the movement of these plates along the fault line, Turkey is one of the most earthquake-

▲ The baking heat of the summer has reduced this river, a tributary of the Euphrates, to a trickle. The mountains in the background are part of the Anti-Taurus range, located in southeastern Anatolia.

TURKEY'S CLIMATE

The diversity of landscapes across the country results in marked differences of climate from one region to another. In particular, the coastal mountain ranges have an effect on the climate inland. The Aegean and Mediterranean coasts have Mediterranean climates, with cool, wet

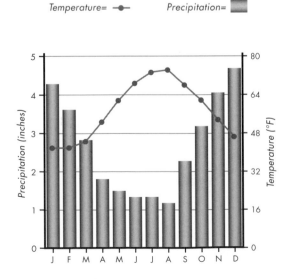

▲ Average monthly climate conditions in Istanbul.

prone places in the world. Earthquakes often occur in groups over a number of years, moving either eastward or westward along the fault. For example, between 1939 and 1944, several major earthquakes moved gradually westward along the fault. The 1939 earthquake devastated the city of Erzincan, causing more than 30,000 deaths. After the Izmit earthquake of 1999, experts are worried that the next big earthquake could hit Istanbul directly.

Focus on: The Izmit Earthquake

On the night of August 17, 1999, a huge earthquake struck northwest Turkey. With its epicenter near the town of Gölcük, the effects of the earthquake were felt as far east as the city of Düzce, and in Istanbul. The earthquake measured 7.4 on the Richter scale, and it lasted for 45 seconds. Official figures put the number of people it killed at over 17,000, although many unofficial estimates are much higher than that. The earthquake hit one of the most densely populated and industrialized regions of the country. Thousands of concrete apartment buildings collapsed during the earthquake, trapping and killing their occupants. In the aftermath, it was found that many of these buildings were not properly constructed, in spite of laws that are supposed to ensure that buildings are made to survive a major earthquake.

▼ This house was completely destroyed by the earthquake that hit Gölcük on August 17, 1999. The town's mosque (rear) withstood the shaking.

CHAPTER 4

Population and Settlements

Turkey has a population of about 73 million people. Its rate of population growth, which increased through much of the 20th century, has decreased sharply in recent decades, largely as a result of better education about family planning and increased use of contraception. In 1971, the fertility rate was an average of 5.9 babies per woman. By 2005, this rate had dropped to 1.92 babies per woman.

TURKEY'S PEOPLE

About 80 percent of the population is ethnically Turkish. An estimated 17 percent are of Kurdish origin, and there are also groups of Arabs, Armenians, Greeks, and Jews. The official language of the country is Turkish, but many Kurds speak Kurdish, and the population also includes Arabic, Armenian, and Greek speakers.

? Did You Know?

About 55,000 Armenians live in Turkey today.

THE ARMENIANS

The Armenians are a people who originally lived in parts of eastern Turkey and in what is now Armenia, as well as in neighboring areas. They were the first people to convert to Christianity as a nation; most Armenians in Turkey and elsewhere now belong to their own independent Orthodox Church. The Armenian people lived without major conflict under Ottoman Turkish rule until the 19th century, when the decline of the Ottoman Empire and the success of Greek and Serbian nationalists led to the emergence of Armenian nationalist movements working for an independent Armenian state. An Armenian uprising in 1894 was crushed with considerable loss of life by the Ottoman authorities. At the outbreak of World War I in 1914, an estimated 1.5 million to 2 million Armenians lived in Turkey, mostly in eastern Anatolia. In this region Ottoman Turkey fought a bitter war against the Russian Empire, and the Russians encouraged the Armenian nationalists.

 ▶ Turkish is the official language of Turkey. This shop in Kayseri sells a type of cured beef (*pastirma*) and salami (*sucuk*) that are specialities of the region.

▶ A Kurdish man tends his goats in southeast Anatolia.

Some Armenians fought against the Ottoman Empire, and there were Armenian uprisings behind the Turkish lines. The Ottoman government saw the Armenians as a threat and, in 1915, ordered the expulsion of the Armenians to Mesopotamia (present-day Iraq). Hundreds of thousands of Armenians died on forced marches; others were killed before they could leave. Accounts of the number of Armenians killed by the Ottomans vary between about 600,000 to over 1,000,000. Today, both Armenians and many people around the world refer to the 1915 attack on the Armenians—one of the bloodiest events in history—as the Armenian Genocide. Turkey's government and most Turks deny that these events were a genocide.

THE KURDS

Kurds make up the largest non-Turkish ethnic group in Turkey. Traditionally, the Kurds have lived in the southeast of Anatolia, near the frontiers with Iraq and Iran where there are also large Kurdish populations. Large numbers of Kurds now live in Istanbul, Ankara, and other Turkish cities. The Kurds have their own language, Kurdish, but its use was banned after the founding of modern Turkey. In spite of the ban, many Kurds continued to speak Kurdish, although attempts to publish or broadcast in Kurdish were usually quickly suppressed by the government. Restrictions on the use of Kurdish in education and the broadcast media were lifted in 2003.

Population Data

- 🗀 Population: 73.2 million
- 🗀 Population 0–14 yrs: 30%
- 🗀 Population 15–64 yrs: 65%
- 🗀 Population 65+ yrs: 5%
- 🗀 Population growth rate: 1.3%
- 🗀 Population density: 242.9 per sq mile/ 93.8 per sq km
- 🗀 Urban population: 66%
- 🗀 Major cities: Istanbul 9,760,000
  Ankara 3,593,000
  Izmir 2,500,000

Source: United Nations and World Bank

WHERE DO PEOPLE LIVE?

The average population density in Turkey is about 243 people per square mile (94 people per square km). Actual population density, however, is closely related to the country's landscape and climate. Settlements are concentrated in the fertile, lowland areas, with the mountainous and plateau areas being relatively sparsely populated. Nearly half of the population of Turkey lives around the Sea of Marmara and along the coastal lowlands stretching eastward along the Black Sea to Zonguldak and southward on the Aegean Sea to Izmir. Around 66 percent of Turkey's population lives in cities, with 34 percent living in rural areas. The number of people living in Turkey's cities has more than doubled in the last 40 years. This trend is expected to continue. Turkey's largest cities are Istanbul, Ankara (the capital), Izmir, and Bursa.

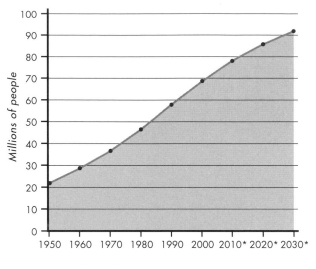

* Projected Population

▲ Population growth 1950–2030

▼ Two-thirds of Turkey's populations lives in cities. In city parks such as this one, picnics are a popular way for a whole family, often including several generations, to get together.

GECEKONDU

The movement of people into Turkey's cities has put considerable strain on urban infrastructure such as housing, water supply, and sanitation. Many new arrivals from the countrysides to cities such as Istanbul and

Ankara live in squatter settlements, known as *gecekondu*, on the outskirts of the cities. The *gecekondu* started as small shelters made from whatever materials could be found that were illegally put up literally overnight. At first, the government tried to control the spread of *gecekondu* by demolishing them and moving their inhabitants. But with no alternative housing available, people continued to build these basic shelters. Today, legislation has been introduced to make many established *gecekondu* legal, and local municipalities have installed services such as drains and water. As the movement of people to Turkey's cities continues, new *gecekondu* continually spring up on their outskirts.

▼ A view of one of the poorer areas of housing in central Ankara in 2006.

Focus on: Istanbul and Ankara

The capital of the Ottoman Empire, Istanbul was considered by Mustafa Kemal to have too many associations with the country's past history to be the capital of the new Republic of Turkey. For this reason, he sited the new capital at the more centrally located city of Ankara. Today, Ankara is Turkey's second biggest city, after Istanbul. It has a population of about 3.6 million, and it is an important commercial and industrial center. With a population of over 9.7 million, Istanbul remains Turkey's largest and most prestigious city. Its Ottoman heritage attracts tourists from all over the world, and its location on the Bosphorus Strait is spectacular.

CHAPTER 5

Government and Politics

Since 1923, Turkey has been a republic. Every year, it celebrates its national day, Republic Day, on October 29. It was under the leadership of Mustafa Kemal that Turkey became a republic and developed into a secular state, with freedom of belief and worship as a central part of its constitution.

▲ Turkish special-force soldiers put on a display in Ankara on Republic Day, October 29, 2005.

GOVERNMENT

Turkey has a parliamentary system of government, with an elected president and a prime minister. Turkey's parliament is called the Turkish Grand National Assembly (TGNA). It has 550 members, known as deputies, who are elected in parliamentary elections. These elections are held every five years, although the TGNA can decide to call an election earlier if necessary. Anyone over the age of 30 who has a minimum of primary school education and who has not been convicted of a serious crime can be elected as a deputy, although there is a campaign to reduce this age limit to 25. All citizens of Turkey over the age of 18 have the right to vote in parliamentary elections.

The TGNA elects a president for one single term of seven years. The president is the head of state and has the power to veto legislation and to return it to the TGNA for further consideration. The president appoints the prime minister, who is usually the leader of the majority party in the TGNA. The prime minister selects ministers who have specific responsibilities such as defense, foreign affairs, the interior, justice, education, public works and housing, health, and transportation.

 Did You Know?

In 1993, Tansu Çiller became Turkey's first female prime minister.

LOCAL GOVERNMENT

The country is divided into 81 provinces that are themselves divided into districts. The provinces are administered by governors who report to the Interior Minister. The governors are appointed by the Council of Ministers. The province governments are responsible for health, public works, education and culture, agriculture, and the economic and commercial sectors. There are also elected municipal governments for the main cities and towns in Turkey. The municipal councils are headed by a mayor, who is elected for a term of five years. The municipal councils are responsible for health, education, transportation systems, and services such as water, sanitation, gas and electricity, and they are authorized to collect municipal taxes. Turkey's smallest local governments are the village assemblies of places with fewer than 2,000 inhabitants. Villagers choose a headman and a council of elders who are responsible for running village finances and for making local decisions about community projects and schools.

POLITICAL PARTIES

The Turkish Republic, initially a one-party state, evolved into a multiparty democracy in 1946, but the military took over on three occasions (1960, 1971, and 1980) when they believed the principles of Atatürk's reforms were threatened. On each occasion, they quickly returned the country to civilian rule, but between the early 1970s and 2002 the country was mostly ruled by a succession of weak minority or coalition governments. The elections in 2002, however, produced an outright winner when the Justice and Development Party (AKP), a party dedicated to Islamic principles that was founded in 2001 by Recep Tayyip Erdogan and Abdullah Gül, swept the board with 363 seats in the TGNA. AKP's opposition was the center-left Republican People's Party (CHP), which won 178 seats.

▼ The TGNA, Turkey's parliament, met in February 2003 to discuss whether to allow U.S. troops to enter Turkey if there was a war with Iraq.

THE ISLAMIST PARTIES

As a result of Atatürk's reforms in the early years of the Republic, Turkey's government is strictly secular. In the recent past, however, Islamist parties have become more powerful in Turkey, drawing their support both from people disillusioned with the other parties and from those who want to see more involvement of Islam in the political system. For many secular Turks, the Islamist parties challenge the secularism of the state. In 1995, the Islamist Welfare Party won a larger proportion of the vote than any other party in the general election and formed a coalition government. It started to strengthen ties with Islamic Middle Eastern countries, as well as proposing measures such as extending Islamic education. Under pressure from the military, the coalition collapsed in 1997, and the Islamist Welfare Party was banned in the following year. The party was reconstituted under a new name but was again closed in 2001. A new party was founded, the Justice and Development Party (AKP), led by the former mayor of Istanbul, Recep Tayyip Erdogan. Although this party is also Islamist, it is more moderate than its predecessors, and it has strengthened ties with the United States and the EU. It has also abolished the death penalty (2002) and challenged the power of the army to influence the country's politics. These changes are part of Turkey's preparation for membership in the EU.

THE PROBLEM OF THE PKK

In the late 1970s, a nationalist Kurdish organization called the Kurdistan Workers' Party (PKK) emerged. The aim of the PKK is to establish an independent state for Kurds in a region that includes southeast Turkey. In the 1980s, the PKK began a campaign of terrorism against Turkey's government, as well as against civilians, particularly in the Kurdish southeast. The PKK targeted government officials and civilians who opposed its activities, leading the government to impose military law in the region. In the 1990s, the PKK attacked tourist sites and kidnapped tourists in an attempt to damage Turkey's tourism industry. In response to the PKK campaign, Turkey's government attacked suspected PKK bases in southeastern Turkey and imposed military law in the region.

◄ Turkey's prime minister, Recep Tayyip Erdogan, waves as he stands in front of a portrait of Atatürk in Ankara in June 2003.

More than 30,000 people are thought to have died in this violence. Turkey was condemned by the European Court of Human Rights and by many countries for abuses of human rights during this period.

In 1999, the leader of the PKK, Abdullah Ocalan, was captured. Ocalan was tried and sentenced to death, although this sentence was changed to life imprisonment in 2002. The arrest of Ocalan resulted in a cease-fire and a call from Ocalan for PKK fighters to surrender their arms. In 2000, the PKK formally

announced the end of violence and that it would campaign peacefully for Kurdish rights in Turkey rather than for a Kurdish homeland. In 2004, however, a reorganized PKK announced the end of the cease-fire. It blamed Turkey's government for not making progress in improving Kurdish rights.

Did You Know?

In 1999, Recep Tayyip Erdogan, then the mayor of Istanbul, was briefly jailed for stirring up religious passions by reciting a militant Islamic poem.

Focus on: Leyla Zana

Turkey may have had a female prime minister—Tansu Çiller—but women still remain under-represented in Turkey's government. One of the small number of women to have become deputies in the TGNA was Leyla Zana, a Kurdish human rights activist. Zana was elected to the TGNA in 1991. But as a result of her speaking in Kurdish in parliament—which, because it was broadcast, was still subject to the ban—and her subsequent defense of Kurdish rights, she was later arrested. In 1994, Zana was sentenced to 15 years in prison. Zana was released in 2004, after the European Court of Human Rights ruled that her trial had been unfair.

◀ In June 2004, Leyla Zana and other Kurdish activists rode on the roof of a coach traveling through the city of Diyarbakir, in southeastern Turkey.

CHAPTER 6

Energy and Resources

Turkey has a wealth of mineral reserves and is a leading producer of minerals such as chromite, from which chromium is obtained; boron, of which it has about 60 percent of world reserves; iron ore; celestite; emery; and feldspar. It also has large reserves of coal, some of which are used in the country's important iron and steel manufacturing industries.

ELECTRICITY GENERATION

Demand for energy has risen dramatically since the 1960s because of the demands of increased urbanization and industrialization. Before that time, many rural people relied on non-commercial sources such as biomass fuels, including firewood and manure, which were burned to produce energy. But the mass migration to cities has led to a rapid increase in the number of people in Turkey needing electrical power, and the state-owned suppliers have struggled to keep up with the demand.

Turkey uses its reserves of coal to generate 22.9 percent of its electricity, but because of the low quality of its coal, this method of generating power is highly polluting. A cleaner form of fuel for generating power is natural gas, which Turkey imports from Russia, Iran, Azerbaijan, Algeria, and Nigeria. The Blue Stream natural gas pipeline, completed in 2002, transports gas 866 miles (1,394 km) from Russia

▲ This power station near Izmit is fueled by coal.

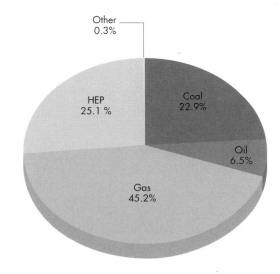

Other 0.3%
HEP 25.1 %
Coal 22.9%
Oil 6.5%
Gas 45.2%

▲ Electricity production by type

to Turkey across the bottom of the Black Sea and is the world's deepest undersea pipeline. Because of its geographical position between Europe and Asia, Turkey is an important potential transit route for gas between these regions. The original agreement for Blue Stream included plans to extend the pipeline to other Mediterranean countries, such as Greece and Italy, although these plans are still under discussion.

OIL

Turkey imports about 90 percent of its oil supply, mainly from the countries of the Middle East and Russia. One major issue is the transport of oil in tankers through the narrow Bosphorus Strait—the location of Turkey's biggest city, Istanbul. Turkey is concerned about the possibility of a major environmental disaster if there was an accident in the narrow

▲ Turkey has some reserves of oil in southeastern Anatolia, the location of this "nodding donkey" oil pump.

strait. The construction of the Baku-Tblisi-Ceyhan oil pipeline, completed in 2005, takes oil 1,100 miles (1,770 km) from Azerbaijan, through Georgia and Turkey, to the Turkish Mediterranean terminal at Ceyhan, bypassing the need to transport the oil through the problematic regions of Iran, Chechnya, and Armenia, and also avoiding the Bosphorus. Other similar pipelines are under consideration for the future.

 Did You Know?

A project to construct Turkey's first nuclear power station was abandoned in 2000 for financial reasons.

RENEWABLE RESOURCES

Turkey's mountainous terrain gives ample opportunity for the construction of dams for hydroelectric power (HEP), and 25.1 percent of the country's electricity is produced by HEP. A project to build more than 20 dams on the Tigris and Euphrates rivers in the southeast of the country, the Southeastern Anatolian Project (Güneydogu Anadolu Projesi, or GAP), started in the 1980s. The aim of the GAP is to harness the waters of the Tigris and Euphrates rivers for power and irrigation and also to help regenerate a poor region through increased agriculture and employment opportunities.

The construction of some of the dams, however, has been controversial. Turkey also has great potential for wind and solar power production, although such renewable resources account for only a tiny amount of the country's energy production at present.

WATER RESOURCES

Although Turkey has greater water resources than many of its Middle Eastern neighbors, it is not a water-rich country. A country is classified as "water rich" if it has supplies of more than 353,000 cubic feet (10,000 cubic meters) of water

Focus on: Southeastern Anatolian Project (GAP)

The GAP is due for completion in 2010, but there has been strong opposition to the construction of some of its dams, particularly from local Kurdish communities. Compensation of those displaced by the dam-building so far has usually been tied to ownership of land or houses. This has resulted in thousands of landless families receiving no compensation at all. It is estimated by

international pressure groups that the flooding that would result from the Ilisu Dam on the Tigris would displace between 15,000 and 20,000 people. It would also flood the ancient city of Hasankeyf, which is of particular historical importance and which has been designated as a nature conservation area by Turkey's government since 1981.

► The huge Atatürk Dam, shown here, is the centerpiece of the Southeast Anatolian Project (GAP).

per person per year, but the average figure for Turkey is well below this, at around 105,900 cubic feet (3,000 cubic meters) per year. Turkey has 26 basins that drain the country's rivers. The largest are the basins of the Tigris and the Euphrates which, between them, account for 28.5 percent of Turkey's total surface water flow. Turkey's climate, however, varies from region to region. While some northern areas receive regular rainfall, other areas are arid. For this reason, the amount of available water for agriculture and other uses varies greatly between regions, and big cities such as Istanbul and Ankara often experience water shortages during the summer months. Nevertheless, Turkey exports water to neighboring water-poor countries. In 2004, the country signed an agreement with Israel to supply it with water from the Manavgat River, which flows into the Mediterranean on the southern coast. The water will be transported in giant water tankers across the eastern Mediterranean.

▲ A farmer opens up irrigation channels near Antalya, on Turkey's Mediterranean coast, to water a field before planting potatoes.

Energy Data

🗁 Energy consumption as % of world total: 0.7%

🗁 Energy consumption by sector (% of total):
   Industry: 31.6%
   Transportation: 23.2%
   Agriculture: 5.7%
   Services: 4.1%
   Residential: 30.8%
   Other: 4.6%

🗁 CO_2 emissions as % of world total: 0.9%

🗁 CO_2 emissions per capita in ton per year: 3.3
   Source: World Resources Institute

CHAPTER 7

Economy and Income

Turkey is a developing country and its economy has become increasingly industrialized since the 1950s. Manufacturing is now more important than agriculture in the country but its economy remains mixed, with cosmopolitan centers of industry, commerce, and trade contrasting with much less developed regions characterized by traditional agriculture. Turkey has a mixture of state- and privately owned companies, with the state playing major roles in the banking, transportation, utilities, and communications sectors.

THE ECONOMY

Turkey began reforms in the 1980s to change from an economy in which the government controlled industry and finance to an economy in which private companies played larger role. Problems with inflation and recessions, however, plagued the economy. During the country's most recent economic crisis, inflation was over 80 percent in the late 1990s, and the banking system, collapsed in 2001. With help from the World Bank and the International Monetary Fund (IMF), Turkey is recovering from this crisis. The country now has a greatly reduced inflation rate and a program of privatization for sectors of the economy such as banking and communications.

Focus on: Inflation

Inflation has been a chronic problem for Turkey's economy. In the late 1990s, Turkey suffered from inflation of over 80 percent, meaning that the cost of basic goods increased by 80 percent every 12 months. At the same time, the value of Turkey's currency, the lira, was decreasing, so people found that the money they had was worth less and less. Strict economic reform has brought the situation under control. In 2004, Turkey's inflation rate went below double figures, to about 8 percent, for the first time for 30 years.

► People walk to work in the modern office buildings of Istanbul.

▲ A wide range of fresh produce is for sale at this busy market in Istanbul.

FARMING

Turkey's abundant arable land is a major resource, particularly along the coastal areas. Turkey is self-sufficient in food, and farming employs 24 percent of male workers and 59 percent of female workers. Agriculture, however, makes up only 13 percent of the country's GDP. About 50 percent of Turkey's cropland is used for growing grains such as wheat, barley, and corn. Tobacco is a major export for Turkey, as are cotton, fruits (grapes, raisins, melons, figs, apricots), vegetables, and nuts (particularly hazelnuts). Many farms remain small and unmechanized, and output varies greatly from region to region depending on the climate.

 Did You Know?

Although Turkey has a long coastline, fishing is not among its major economic activities. Overfishing has depleted its stocks, and its coastal waters are polluted.

Economic Data

- Gross National Income (GNI) in U.S.$: 268,962,000,000
- World rank by GNI: 20
- GNI per capita in U.S.$: 3,750
- World rank by GNI per capita: 89
- Economic growth: 8.9%

Source: World Bank

INDUSTRY AND MANUFACTURING

In the 1920s, Turkey had very few factories. Today, it has thousands catering to the domestic demand for a wide variety of products, as well as a thriving export market. The country's largest industries are in the textile sector, which produces cloth and clothing for home and international markets. This sector makes up 37 percent of Turkey's total of industrial exports. The country also has food and beverage processing industries, and its car manufacturing and electronics industries have become more important in recent years. Many of Turkey's companies are privately owned. For example, Arçelik makes household appliances. Other companies that have factories in Turkey are multinationals. For example, the foreign car manufacturers Fiat, Honda, and Renault all have factories in Turkey.

 Did You Know?

About 2 percent of Turkey's population lives on less than U.S.$1 a day, and 10 percent of the country's people live on less than U.S.$2 a day.

Turkey's heavy industries include oil refining, manufacturing of machinery such as tractors, and production of iron, steel, cement, and fertilizers. Most of this industrial activity is based around the industrial cities in the country's north and west. For example, Bursa is a center of vehicle manufacture, and Izmit has important oil refineries and cement industries.

REGIONAL VARIATIONS

The local economies of the different regions of Turkey vary widely. The region around the Sea of Marmara, which includes Istanbul, Bursa, and Izmit, accounts for about one-third of the country's GDP. Other centers of industry and commerce are the capital, Ankara; Izmir, on the west coast; and the triangular region in the corner of the Mediterranean coast between the cities of Adana, Mersin, and Iskenderun. The southern and western coastal regions are Turkey's richest areas for agriculture and tourism. The country's northern coast, its southeast, and Central Anatolia are all comparatively undeveloped.

▶ An export fair for the textile industry was held in Istanbul in 2006. Turkey is a world leader in the production of textiles and clothes.

These regional variations are reflected in large variations in income. According to figures from the State Institute of Statistics (SIS), over 28 percent of people in Turkey lived in poverty in 2003. The SIS calculates poverty according to the local cost of a selection of basic needs, including nonfood items. According to this measure, Turkey's number of people living in poverty is rising—in spite of the expansion of the country's economy—because while prices have risen, wages have stayed low. Poverty is acute in many rural regions, particularly the southeast, but it is also a problem in urban slum areas. Turkey's government is addressing the problems of poverty and deprivation in the southeast through the Southeastern Anatolian Project. The project has increased the amount of arable land in the region through irrigation, but it also has wider aims including bringing improved health and education to the region.

◄ This aluminum smelter is in the industrial town of Gebze, near Istanbul.

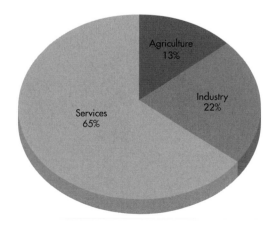

▲ Contribution by sector to national income

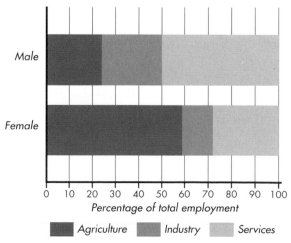

Percentage of total employment

Agriculture   Industry   Services

▲ Labor force by sector and gender

CHAPTER 8

Global Connections

Turkey's role in the world and relationship with other countries is largely influenced by its unique geographical location between Asia and Europe. Since ancient times, the region has been strategically important. Today, guided by the principles laid down by Mustafa Kemal Atatürk when the Turkish Republic was founded, Turkey follows a policy of "Peace at home and Peace abroad" in its dealings with foreign countries.

TURKEY AND THE EU

Turkey started its relationship with the European Union when it applied for full membership in the European Economic Community (EEC, the forerunner of the EU) in 1987. During the 1990s, trade between the EU and Turkey increased as Turkey gradually removed import restrictions. In 1999, Turkey was accepted as a candidate for EU membership, but was told that it needed to make progress on human rights issues and economic reforms. As part of a package of reforms aimed at EU membership, Turkey abolished the death penalty in 2002 and introduced tougher measures against torture. The Turkish government has also given more civil rights to its Kurdish population, such as the right to broadcast in the Kurdish language, although such broadcasts are still subject to tight restrictions. Turkey's relationship with Cyprus is another major hurdle to its EU membership. In 2004, negotiations led to an agreement that Turkey would recognize the

▼ Members of the EU parliament in Strasbourg vote after a debate on Turkey's membership in the EU in September 2005.

Focus on: Cyprus

The Turkish Republic of Northern Cyprus covers the northern one-third of the Mediterranean island of Cyprus. It is recognized as a state only by Turkey. All other countries recognize only the sovereignty of the Republic of Cyprus (which controls the southern part of the island). In 2004, Kofi Annan, the secretary-general of the United Nations, put forward a proposal to reunify the island. Known as the Annan plan, it proposed joining the Greek and Turkish Cypriot sectors to create a United Cyprus Republic. A referendum was held on the plan in 2004, but while 65 percent of the Turkish Cypriot population accepted it, 75 percent of the Greek Cypriot population rejected it.

▼ Greek and Turkish leaders meet for talks with the secretary-general of the United Nations, Kofi Annan (center), in May 2002.

Republic of Cyprus as an EU member before membership talks began in 2005. This did not happen before the talks started, although pressure continues to be exerted on Turkey to take this step and to implement an agreement the country made in 2005 to open its ports to Greek Cypriot ships.

There are several issues surrounding Turkey's joining the EU. Many EU countries are concerned that Turkey will become the EU's most populous member when its population overtakes that of Germany, which is currently the most populated EU state. Other concerns center on Turkey's human rights record, as well as cultural and religious differences. Some states, such as Britain and Germany, are firmly in support of Turkey's joining, while others, such as France and Austria, are more skeptical and plan to hold referendums on the question.

GLOBAL RELATIONSHIPS

Turkey has a close relationship with the United States. Turkey was an ally of the United States during the Cold War, fought with the United Nations forces in the Korean War, and was a member of the coalition that liberated Kuwait in the 1991 Gulf War. Turkey's refusal to give U.S. troops access to Iraq across its territories in 2003, however, cooled the relationship and led to the canceling of a major aid package by the United States. Official visits in 2004 of Turkey's prime minister, Recep Tayyip Erdogan, to Washington, D.C., and of U.S. president George W. Bush to Turkey, have helped to restore the ties between the two countries. The United States is a strong supporter of Turkey's membership in the EU.

Turkey also has important relationships with many of the republics of the former Soviet Union, particularly Azerbaijan. Turkey's relations with Russia have improved in recent years, resulting in an increase in trade and projects such as the Blue Stream gas pipeline. Relations between Turkey and Greece have also improved since 1999, causing benefits in trade and tourism. Turkey is a member of the North Atlantic Treaty Organization (NATO) and has the second-largest armed forces of any NATO member. Turkey contributes troops to both NATO and UN peacekeeping operations all around the world, as well as keeping a force in Turkish Cyprus.

WORLD TRADE

Turkey has been a member of the World Trade Organization (WTO) since 1995, and the country has important trade links with countries all around the world. Chief imports into Turkey include chemicals, machinery, and oil. Turkey's main exports are clothing and textiles, iron and steel, foods such as fruit and nuts, construction materials, vehicles, and appliances. The majority of Turkey's exports go to EU countries, although the United States, the Middle Eastern countries, and Turkey's other neighbors are all important export markets.

 Did You Know?

Nearly 2 million Turks live and work in Germany.

◀ A Turkish soldier guards a NATO aircraft in Konya, located in central Turkey, in 2003.

Focus on: Turks Abroad

In 2004, there were about 3.5 million Turks living and working abroad, mostly in Western Europe. Turkish workers began to go to Western Europe to find work in the 1960s. Although some Turks went to the Netherlands, Austria, and France, the vast majority moved to West Germany, which invited workers from Turkey to meet labor shortages. After the reunification of West Germany and East Germany in 1989, high unemployment rates in the country led to calls for Turkish "guest workers" to return home. In some extreme cases, there were attacks on the Turkish community in Germany. Many Turks, however, have made their homes in Germany. Turkish people also work in Middle Eastern countries such as Saudi Arabia, and there are

Turkish communities in Britain and the United States. Many Turks send money back to their families in Turkey. In 2000, money sent home by Turks working in other countries amounted to U.S.$4.5 billion.

▼ Turkish workers buy food at a Turkish delicatessen in Berlin, Germany.

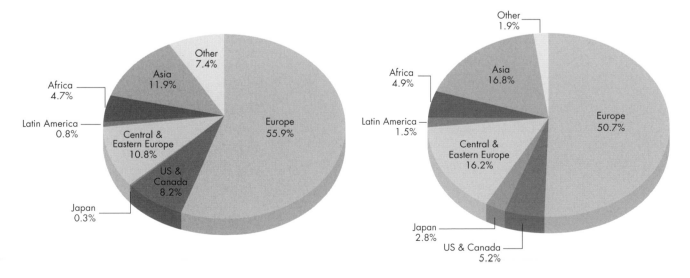

▲ Destination of exports by major trading region

▲ Origin of imports by major trading region

CHAPTER 9

Transportation and Communications

Turkey's geographical position between east and west means that its transportation infrastructure is vitally important for the development of the region as a whole. In addition to having an important role in world trade, Turkey is used as a transit country for goods. However, low investment and Turkey's often mountainous terrain have slowed the development of Turkey's transportation systems in many areas.

ROAD AND RAIL

In 2004, Turkey had 96,197 miles (154,807 km) of paved roads and 119,772 miles (192,747 km) of unpaved roads. The country's main highways are centered around its major cities, including

Transport & Communications Data

- Total roads: 215,969 miles/347,553 km
- Total paved roads: 96,197 miles/ 154,807 km
- Total unpaved roads: 119,772 miles/ 192,747 km
- Total railways: 5,404 miles/8,697 km
- Airports: 117
- Cars per 1,000 people: 66
- Cellular phones per 1,000 people: 484
- Personal computers per 1,000 people: 52
- Internet users per 1,000 people: 142

Source: World Bank and CIA World Factbook

◀ Traffic congestion in Istanbul. The city's road traffic increases by an estimated 500 vehicles daily.

Focus on: The Akbil

In Istanbul, people are being encouraged to use the city's public transportation system in order to try to alleviate the city's chronic traffic congestion. To make this easier, the Akbil system—an integrated ticket system that allows people to travel by bus, tram, ferry, subway or overground train without having to buy different tickets— was introduced. An Akbil is a piece of plastic no bigger than a key with a metal button at one end. Inside the button is a computer chip. On every trip, the passenger presses the button into a circular socket that deducts the fare for that trip. People can buy fares or "recharge" their Akbils at bus, subway, and train stations, as well as at Akbil kiosks throughout the city. The program has been a great success, and people can now even use Akbils to buy drinks from vending machines.

▶ A passenger uses his Akbil to go through a turnstile for the tram network in Istanbul.

Ankara, Istanbul, Izmir, and Adana. Many of these roads are three-lane highways built to international standards. The government is investing in a program of highway-building to improve links between its major cities, such as the toll road that now links Ankara and Istanbul and a highway between Istanbul and Izmir. In 2004, there were about 4.8 million cars on Turkey's roads (about 66 cars for every 1,000 people). The growth of urbanization is one of the factors in Turkey's massive increase in car ownership and road use. Hand-in-hand with this growth, however, is an increase in the number of road accidents. Turkey's traffic accident rate is between three and six times higher than that of the European Union.

The country's government is working to try to reduce the number of fatalities on its roads.

In 2004, Turkey had 5,404 miles (8,697 km) of railway, linking the country's major cities. Rail travel is relatively slow and inefficient, and, as a result, it is not very popular. Only 2 percent of Turkey's passenger transport was by rail in 2003. A new high-speed rail link between Ankara and Istanbul is under construction. It will reduce the time for this trip from over six hours to about three hours. Other rail projects include a new rail link between Ankara and Konya and an underground rail system to link up the European and Asian sides of Istanbul beneath the Bosphorus (the Marmaray Project).

BUS AND *DOLMUS*

Bus services travel between all of Turkey's major cities and are a popular and fairly cheap way to travel. Some journeys are very long. The bus from Istanbul to Artvin, in the far northeast of the country, covers 840 miles (1,352 km) and takes 24 hours. A *dolmus* is a kind of shared taxi that operates within cities and between cities and nearby towns. Every *dolmus* runs along a particular route, and a *dolmus* car or minibus leaves for its destination when all (or nearly all) of its seats are full. Each passenger pays a proportion of the fare, making it a much cheaper option than a normal taxi.

AIRPORTS AND PORTS

Turkey has 89 airports with paved runways. The country's main airports are in Istanbul, Ankara, and Izmir. The national airline is Turkish Airlines, and it flies to places around the world. Domestic flights are operated by Turkish Airlines and by budget airlines such as Atlas Jet and Onur Air. Turkey's main ports are Istanbul, Mersin, Izmir, and Iskenderun.

MEDIA AND COMMUNICATIONS

Turkey's telecommunications system was updated and expanded in the 1980s and early 1990s. Today, there are nearly 19 million telephone lines in use in the country. The system continues to be updated with fiber-optic and digital links between major cities and satellite links in more remote regions. The number of cellular phones has grown rapidly, and, in 2004, over 35 million cell phones were in use in Turkey. Turkey's number of Internet users has also grown from about 2 million in 2000 to over 10 million in 2004.

Turkey has 35 daily newspapers, most of which are based in Istanbul but also printed and distributed from Ankara and Izmir. The country's wide range of newspapers represents many different viewpoints, from Islamist, at one extreme, to liberal and left wing, at the

▼ Izmir, one of Turkey's major ports, has busy container docks.

▲ A young couple catch up on the latest news. Turkey has a wide range of newspapers.

other. There is, however, some government control over the media. In particular, Article 301 of Turkey's penal code makes it a crime to insult "being a Turk, the Republic, or Turkish Grand National Assembly . . . ." In 2005, this Article was used to prosecute novelist Orhan Pamuk when he reportedly told a Swiss newspaper that "one million Armenians were killed in these lands and nobody but me dares to talk about it." Pamuk later denied using the word "genocide" in relation to the Armenian killings. The charges against Pamuk were dropped in 2006.

Turkey has a national publicly funded broadcasting company, the Turkish Radio and Television Corporation (TRT), which was the only provider of radio and television before the early 1990s, when the market was deregulated to allow commercial channels. Today, TRT has domestic channels covering news, sports, music, and current affairs, as well as several radio channels. A wide range of satellite and cable channels are also available around the country. In 2003, under pressure from the EU, Turkey's government began allowing a very restricted amount of broadcasting in Kurdish.

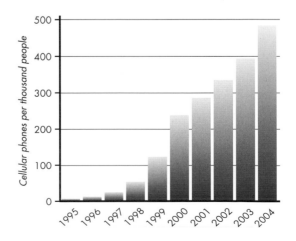

▲ Cellular phone use 1995–2004

CHAPTER 10

Education and Health

Turkey's education system was completely reformed in the early years of the Republic, when the religious schools were closed and replaced with secular schools. Today, education is a high priority for Turkey's government.

In 1997, Turkey's government extended compulsory education from five to eight years. Turkish children start their primary education the age of seven and must attend school until they are 15. While nearly all boys attend school, enrollment for girls is lower, particularly in rural areas. One result is that although Turkey has a high literacy rate (nearly 98 percent), the rate for men is higher than that for women. Children usually have the same teacher throughout their primary school years. Classes are often big—up to 50 pupils—but the government is making

efforts to reduce class sizes. After five years of primary school, children move to middle schools where they have a different teacher for each subject. In recent years, Turkey's schools have emphasized teaching foreign languages and computer skills in these schools.

About 58 percent of Turkey's students continue with their education at high schools. At this level, there are different schools to choose from, including Anatolian high schools, where some lessons are taught in a foreign language; science and social science schools; religious *imam hatip okullari*; and vocational schools that educate students for jobs in areas such as tourism, industry, or agriculture.

▼ A teacher leads a class of children in a primary school in Istanbul.

HIGHER EDUCATION

In order to progress to one of Turkey's universities, students have to pass the national university entrance exam. There are about 80 universities in Turkey. Founded over 500 years ago, Istanbul University is the oldest university in the country. It was the only institution of higher education when the Turkish Republic was founded, so it has played a role in training and helping to set up other universities in the country. Education at government-funded universities is free. The country also has private universities that charge fees.

 Did You Know?

After the founding of the Turkish Republic, religious schools were closed, and the school curriculum no longer included religious studies. In 1949, religious education was reintroduced in Turkey's primary schools on a voluntary basis. In addition, religious high schools, called *imam hatip okullari*, were set up in the 1950s to train imams, or Islamic religious leaders.

▲ The main entrance to Istanbul University, the oldest and largest university in Turkey.

Focus on: Headscarves

The issue of women's clothing has caused great controversy in Turkey's educational institutions. In the 1980s, some female students began to wear headscarves to show their commitment to their religion. The wearing of headscarves is banned in schools and universities. Those in favor of the ban see the wearing of headscarves as a political statement challenging the secular nature of the Turkish Republic. Those in favor of headscarves see it as a matter of personal choice and liberty. This issue is still hotly debated throughout Turkey.

Education and Health

- Life expectancy at birth male: 68.8
- Life expectancy at birth female: 71.1
- Infant mortality rate per 1,000: 33
- Under five mortality rate per 1,000: 39
- Physicians per 1,000 people: 1.4
- Health expenditure as % of GDP: 7.6%
- Education expenditure as % of GDP: 3.6%
- Primary-school net enrollment: 88%
- Student-teacher ratio, primary: n/a
- Adult literacy as % age 15+: 97.7

Source: United Nations Agencies and World Bank

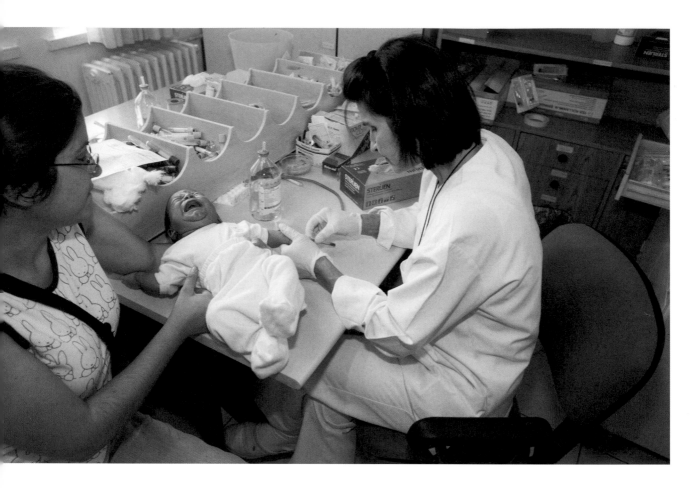

▲ A doctor takes a blood sample from a baby in a hospital in Kayseri, in central Turkey.

HEALTH CARE

Health care in Turkey is largely provided by the Ministry of Health. Other organizations, such as the Ministry of Defense, universities, and the Social Insurance Organization (SSK), also run hospitals, resulting in a fragmented health-care system. In 2003, Turkey's spending on health care was 7.6 percent of the country's GDP (compared to 8 percent of GDP in Britain and 15.2 percent in the United States). This percentage amounted to health-care spending of U.S.$528 per person, counting money spent both privately and by the government. This figure compares to U.S.$2,389 in Britain and U.S.$5,711 in the United States.

Health care coverage in Turkey is uneven, with the best facilities in the densely populated areas of the west, while rural areas tend to be less well served. Basic services are provided at health posts and health centers. In 2002, there were 11,735 health posts in villages across Turkey, each one serving a rural population of between 1,000 and 2,000 people. There were 5,840 health centers in urban areas, each one serving a population of between 5,000 and 10,000. While health posts are staffed by a midwife, health centers have a staff that includes a doctor, nurse, and midwife. Their main function is general patient care—including immunizations, maternal and child health, and family planning—as well as health data collection. Emergency care is provided by a nationwide ambulance service to take people to the nearest hospital. In some remote, rural areas, however, people are more often transported by private vehicle to the nearest large city for treatment.

For the majority of Turkey's population, the cost of health care is covered by a national insurance program which is paid for by taxes. Many people who can afford it also have private health care insurance, and many doctors work in both the private and state sectors. The Social Insurance Organization (SSK) is a social security organization for employees, providing both health care and pensions. In 2004, nearly 50 percent of all hospital beds in Turkey were provided by the Ministry of Health in its 708 hospitals. The next largest providers were the SSK with 148 hospitals and the universities with 50 hospitals. Health care in Turkey's university hospitals and other private hospitals is reputed to be of the highest standard in the country.

The most frequently reported causes of death in Turkey include infectious diseases such as rubella (German measles) and dysentery, heart disease (particularly among people over age 45), and cancer. While diseases such as typhoid fever have decreased since the 1980s as a result of improved access to clean water, cases of malaria are on the increase, particularly in the southeast of the country. Turkey has a low incidence of HIV/AIDS, with 1,922 HIV cases reported in the period between 1985 and 2004.

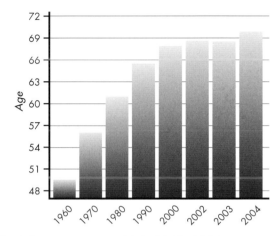

▲ Life expectancy at birth 1960–2004

▼ An ambulance delivers a patient to a hospital in Kayseri.

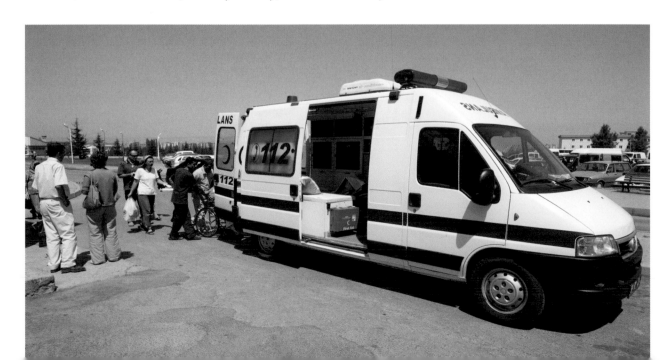

CHAPTER 11

Culture and Religion

In Turkish society, family life is very important. The extended family plays a major role in both urban and rural settings. As well as providing care for elderly family members, or support at times such as the birth of a baby or sickness, the extended family is also important economically. Family businesses often involve several generations of the same family, while in rural areas, extended families often work together to farm their land.

HONOR KILLINGS

Hand-in-hand with the importance of family goes a strong sense of family honor. Particularly in the rural areas of the east and southeast, members of the family, especially the female members, are expected to uphold family honor at all times. Behavior that is considered to bring dishonor can have drastic consequences. It is estimated that every year in Turkey, at least 60 women are murdered by their families in so-called "honor killings." In the past, the traditional concept of honor could be used as a defense for men accused of murdering a female relative. This defense is no longer legal in Turkey, and the government has introduced tough penalties to try to bring an end to the practice of honor killing. A survey in 2005 by a Turkish university found, however, that the traditional concept of honor is still deeply

 Did You Know?

Turkish men over the age of 20 must do 15 months of service in the Turkish armed forces (university graduates and Turks living abroad can serve for shorter periods).

▲ A bride and groom get into a taxi on a busy street in Ankara. Modern Western-style weddings are growing in popularity in Turkey.

entrenched in rural Turkish society. The researchers also found that 37 percent of the men questioned in the Kurdish southeast of the country thought that the appropriate punishment for a woman who had committed adultery was death.

FOOD AND DRINK

Turkish hospitality is an age-old tradition, with food and drink playing a central role. Turkey has a rich and varied cuisine, based on the wide variety of food that is produced in the country's rich agricultural regions. Turkey's history also plays a part in its cuisine, because the many different cultures that came under the rule of the Ottoman Empire all contributed to the combinations of foods and tastes that today make up Turkish cuisine. Staples of the Turkish diet are many types of bread, vegetables, yogurt, and, in coastal regions, fish. The best-known meat dish is kebab, or chunks of meat on a skewer that are grilled or cooked in an oven. The main drinks are coffee and tea, often accompanied by delicious sweet pastries. Although the population of Turkey is largely Muslim, many people in the country ignore the Islamic prohibition against alcohol. Those Turks who do drink alcohol usually do so while eating a meal. Taverns called *meyhane* serve alcoholic drinks with small savory dishes, called *mezes*, such as stuffed peppers and vine leaves and hummus. Some—but by no means all—restaurants hold licenses to serve alcoholic drinks.

▶ A man slices meat from a revolving grill to make a *döner* kebab.

ARTS AND LITERATURE

Atatürk considered culture to be a vital element in the new Turkish Republic, and there is a lively arts scene in the country today. Turkey has rich traditions of music and dance to draw on, resulting in a wide variety of performing arts, including modern rock and pop music, traditional Turkish folk music, and the music of the Alevis (Muslims who belong to Turkey's largest religious group after the majority Sunni Muslims). Turkey also has a long tradition of literature, including both poetry and prose. Well-known Turkish writers today include Orhan Pamuk, who won the Nobel Prize for Literature in 2006 for books such as *The Black Book* (1990), *My Name is Red* (1998), and *Snow* (2002). Another well-known Turkish novelist is Yashar Kemal, who achieved worldwide fame with his first novel *Ince Memed (Memed, My Hawk),* which was published in 1955.

ARCHITECTURE

Turkey's long and varied history has left it with a rich architectural heritage. The country's buildings range from the caravanserais, or inns, built across the region to accommodate travelers during Seljuk and Ottoman times, to the magnificent Ottoman mosques in Istanbul, Edirne, and Bursa. As the capital of the Ottoman Empire, Istanbul is particularly rich in Ottoman

Focus on: Traditional handicrafts

Rugs are one of the best-known products of Turkey. The art of weaving rugs has been handed down through generations for centuries, and traditional methods and styles are still used today. There are two main types of rug: carpets are hand-knotted with a pile on one side, while *kilims* are flat woven. Rugs are usually made from wool, although silk and cotton are also used. The Ottoman rulers supported a wide range of skilled craftworkers who produced beautiful tilework, stunning textiles and intricate metalwork. These crafts are still practiced, for example in the copperware that is used in many Turkish households.

► A woman weaves a rug on a loom in a small workshop in Istanbul. Each region of Turkey has a distinctive style of weaving and many women move from rural areas to find better-paid work using their traditional skills in Istanbul. Handmade rugs from Turkey are sold worldwide.

architecture. Examples include the Topkapi Palace, the Süleymaniye Mosque, and the villas (*yali*) that overlook the Bosphorus.

RELIGION IN TURKEY

Turkey is officially a secular country, and the country's constitution guarantees religious freedom. However, more than 97 percent of Turks are Muslims. Most are Sunni Muslims, although there is a large population of Alevis, who are Muslims who belong to the Shi'a branch of Islam but who are liberal in their religious practice. There are other small religious groups in Turkey, including Christians of the Greek Orthodox, Arab Orthodox, Armenian Orthodox, Syrian Orthodox, Catholic, and Protestant denominations, and Jews. All of these groups have freedom to worship. The separation of religion and politics in Turkey is hotly debated between secularists and those who wish to observe traditional Islamic practices.

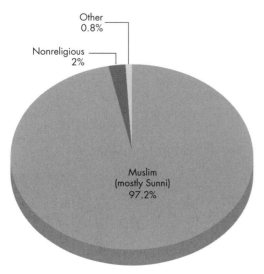

Other
0.8%

Nonreligious
2%

Muslim
(mostly Sunni)
97.2%

▲ Turkey's major religions

► The Hagia Sophia, located in Istanbul, was built as a Christian church. It later became a mosque. Today, it is a museum.

CHAPTER 12

Leisure and Tourism

Traditionally, many Turkish men spend their leisure time in coffee houses playing card games or backgammon. Soccer is very popular, and all over Turkey men and boys kick soccer balls around the streets and on improvised soccer fields. Turkey's national team won third place in the 2002 World Cup, although it failed to qualify for the 2006 World Cup. The best-known soccer teams in Turkey are Galatasaray, Fenerbahçe, and Besiktas, all based in Istanbul. Many Turkish soccer players play for top teams such as Inter Milan and Parma.

▼ Men play board games and drink coffee in outdoor cafés like this one in Osmaniye in Turkey's southeast.

Other popular sports in Turkey include weightlifting, track-and-field sports, and basketball. In August 2005, Turkey hosted its first Grand Prix race. The race featured the opening of a new specially built Formula 1 racing track in Istanbul.

Some popular sports in Turkey are less well-known. Grease- or oil-wrestling dates back to Ottoman times, when it became established as a sport. It still attracts large crowds across the country, with the biggest gathering in Edirne at the end of June. Two men dressed in leather shorts, called *kispet*, cover themselves in olive oil before starting to wrestle. The wrestlers, or *pehlivan*, try to grab their opponent's *kispet* in order to gain control of the match.

▲ Sofular Hamami is one of the oldest *hamams*, or Turkish baths, in Istanbul. It dates back to the 16th century.

Another traditional Turkish sport is *cirit*, or javelin-throwing. This equestrian sport originated with the Seljuks and is still celebrated at festivals in eastern Turkey, such as the Cirit Games that are held every week in the summer in Erzurum. The game is played between two teams of mounted players who aim their javelins—rubber-ended wooden poles about 3 feet (1 m) long—at their opponents in a test of speed, skill, and horsemanship.

HAMAMS

The tradition of public baths in Turkey extends back to Roman times. Until the middle of the 20th century, when Western-style bathrooms began to be built in Turkish homes, the *hamams,* or baths, were the only means of bathing for most Turks. They were also important social centers. In the past, the *hamam* was often a place for celebration of a particular event, such as the preparations for a girl's wedding day. Today, every town in Turkey still has at least one *hamam*, and many Turks continue to visit the *hamam* regularly for a steam bath and a massage. Both men and women visit a *hamam*, although at different times. In cities such as Istanbul, sumptuous *hamams* survive from the Ottoman era.

 Did You Know?

Camel wrestling is a popular spectator sport in the Aegean region of Turkey. Two trained male camels butt and lean on each other, until one of them runs away. Often spectators have to leap out of the running camel's path!

◀ The beach and hotels at Gölenye, in Marmaris on the Aegean coast of Turkey, draw many vacationers.

TOURISM

Tourism is a hugely important and growing industry in Turkey. In 2004, nearly 17 million tourists visited the country, mostly from Europe and Russia. Tourism plays a vital role in Turkey's economy and employs 1.5 million people in the country. Its importance is reflected in the government's emphasis on improving infrastructure, services, and tourist attractions. The aim is to increase the number of tourists visiting Turkey to 30 million a year by 2010.

TOURIST ATTRACTIONS

Thanks to its long history and its geographical location, Turkey is a country rich in fascinating ancient sites. Tourists come to visit the archaeological excavations at Troy, Pergamum, and Ephesus. Turkey also boasts some extraordinary geological features—notably the rock formations of Cappadocia, located in central Anatolia, where the wind and rain have eroded the soft volcanic rock into strange pillar shapes known as "fairy chimneys." For many hundreds of years, people have carved out homes in these rock pillars. They created huge networks of underground and cave homes. In medieval times, churches were also carved out of this rock. Further west, in the Aegean region, people can visit the ruins of the ancient city of Hierapolis, which lie next to another geological wonder, the white limestone terraces of Pamukkale ("cotton castle"). The terraces are almost 300 feet (90 m) high. They formed from deposits left by the mineral-rich water that flows down the hillside. Many beautiful beaches on the Aegean and Mediterranean coasts attract both local and international tourists.

Tourism in Turkey

- 🗁 Tourist arrivals, millions: 16.826
- 🗁 Earnings from tourism in U.S.$: n/a
- 🗁 Tourism as % foreign earnings: n/a
- 🗁 Tourist departures, millions: 7.299
- 🗁 Expenditure on tourism in U.S.$: n/a

Source: World Bank

Istanbul is one of the great cities of the world and is a major tourist attraction in its own right. Its long history under the Roman, Byzantine, and Ottoman empires has left a legacy of famous landmarks. One of the best-known landmarks in Istanbul is the Hagia Sophia (Aya Sofia). The Hagia Sophia was built by the Emperor Justinian in A.D. 537, and it was the largest church in the Christian world for nearly one thousand years, before it was converted into a mosque by the Ottomans in 1453. Today, it is a museum. Built in the early 1600s to rival the Hagia Sophia, the Sultanahmet Mosque is one of the most famous Islamic buildings in the world. It is called "the blue mosque" because of its blue tilework.

► A tourist explores the "fairy chimneys" of Cappadocia. These strange rock formations have been hollowed out to make homes and churches.

Focus on: Ephesus

Ephesus lies on Turkey's Aegean coast, and it is one of the world's greatest archaeological sites. Under the Romans, the city became a bustling center for trade and commerce, as well as an intellectual and philosophical center. Its Temple of Artemis was one of the Seven Wonders of the Ancient World. Today, one of its most impressive ruins is the facade of the Library of Celsus. Built in A.D. 110–135, it was later damaged by warfare and earthquakes. Ephesus also became a center for Christianity, because it was visited by St. Paul and St. John. According to legend, the Virgin Mary came to Ephesus under the protection of St. John and spent the last years of her life in a small stone house that is now revered by both Christians and Muslims.

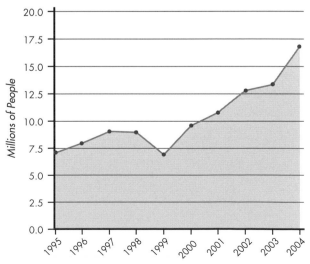

▲ Changes in international tourism 1995–2004

CHAPTER 13

Environment and Conservation

The rapid growth of Turkey's economy and the country's increase in industrialization have raised many environmental issues. Higher levels of energy consumption and increased water and air pollution have all had an impact upon the environment. Turkey set up a Ministry of Environment in 1991, and prospective membership in the European Union has forced the country's government to focus increasingly on environmental issues.

THE BOSPHORUS

One of the major issues for Turkey is marine pollution, specifically the threat of a major oil spill in the Bosphorus or in the Sea of Marmara. In 1994, a Greek Cypriot tanker, the *Nassia*, was involved in a collision in the Bosphorus. The tanker blew up, spilling tons of oil into the water and killing 30 of its crew. The fire raged for five days before it was brought under control, but luckily the accident happened north of the main part of Istanbul. About 50,000 ships pass through the narrow, winding Bosphorus Strait every year, many of them oil tankers, and there is constant pressure on Turkey's government from Black Sea countries to increase the flow of traffic. It is hoped that the construction of transinternational oil pipelines will help to reduce the likelihood of a serious oil spill in the strait.

▼ Pollution from an oil refinery fills the air at Derince, near Istanbul, in 2006.

Focus on: The Black Sea

Turkey has 870 miles (1,400 km) of Black Sea coastline and is, therefore, one of the countries concerned with the problems of marine pollution in this sea. The Black Sea is up to 7,257 feet (2,212 m) deep, and drains an area of about 772,000 sq miles (2 million sq km) from 17 countries. It is almost landlocked, its only outlet being through the Bosphorus Strait to the Sea of Marmara. It is also very vulnerable to eutrophication. Eutrophication is the process by which plant nutrients carried by runoff from the land encourage the rapid growth of phytoplankton in the water, and the phytoplankton starve other organisms of light and oxygen, killing all other life in the water. To combat pollution problems in the Black Sea, Turkey is working with other countries in the region on a Black Sea Strategic Action Plan, partly supported and funded by the United Nations and the World Bank.

▶ The coastline of the Black Sea, near Trabzon, shows signs of oil pollution.

AIR POLLUTION

Air pollution in Turkey is a problem that has resulted from increased energy consumption, industrialization, and car use. In cities such as Istanbul and Ankara, air pollution used to be particularly acute in winter, when smog covered the cities as a result of the low-grade coal people burned to heat their homes. Since the 1990s, however, legislation has been introduced to control the quality of coal and reduce emissions. The country's problems of traffic congestion remain. The slow development of public transportation in Turkey's main cities has done little to reduce the increasing number of vehicles filling their roads.

SOIL EROSION

Much of Turkey is suffering from serious desertification as a result of soil erosion, a problem that affects an estimated 90 percent of Turkey's land. Soil erosion is caused by overgrazing and overfertilization of land, as well as deforestation. Precious topsoil is being degraded as its fertility and ability to absorb water declines and as it is washed away into rivers and reservoirs. An organization called TEMA (Turkish Foundation for Combating Soil Erosion for Reforestation and the Protection of Natural Habitats) has been working since 1992 to raise awareness of this problem and to help people combat these problems at a local level through rural development projects.

interest, as well as places where it is important to protect the biodiversity of a region. They include wetlands such as the Bird Paradise national park, on Manyas Lake near the southern shores of the Sea of Marmara; mountain areas such as Ararat, in the far east of the country; and Gallipoli National Historic Park, on the Gallipoli peninsula between the Aegean and the Dardanelles, the site of a historic campaign in World War I.

ECOTOURISM

Turkey's Ministry of Culture and Tourism has identified ecotourism as an important way to develop Turkey's tourist industry in the future. Because of its wide variety of landscapes and wildlife, Turkey has great potential for activities such as botany (the study of plants), bird-watching, trekking, cycling, water sports, and fishing. Groups such as the World Wildlife Fund (WWF) are working with Turkey's government to protect the country's

▲ This soil in Anatolia is eroded and dried-up. The loss of topsoil is a serious problem in Turkey.

CONSERVATION

Turkey has extremely diverse wildlife. The country also has a wide variety of plants. Among the large mammals to be found in Turkey are the gray wolf, jackal, brown bear, European wild cat, Eurasian lynx, wild boar, gazelle, and chamois. Hunting, deforestation, urban development, and fragmentation of habitats, however, have all played a part in decreasing the numbers of these animals. Since 1958, Turkey's government has created 35 national parks, as well as many other smaller nature preserves. Turkey's national parks include areas of archaeological and historical

Environmental and Conservation Data

- Forested area as % total land area: 9.7%
- Protected area as % total land area: 2.6%
- Number of protected areas: 427

SPECIES DIVERSITY

Category	Known species	Threatened species
Mammals	116	17
Breeding birds	278	11
Reptiles	133	12
Amphibians	23	3
Fish	162	22
Plants	8,650	3

Source: World Resources Institute

environment and promote tourism in places such as the Kure Mountains, in the western Black Sea region of the country, and in some coastal areas. The importance of tourism to Turkey's economy means that its coastal areas are under threat from unchecked development.

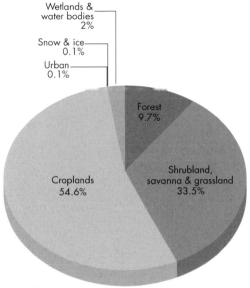

Wetlands & water bodies 2%

Snow & ice 0.1%

Urban 0.1%

Forest 9.7%

Shrubland, savanna & grassland 33.5%

Croplands 54.6%

▲ Types of habitat

 Did You Know?

In 2005, Turkey renamed three animals to avoid references to Kurdistan and Armenia, claiming the names were against "Turkish unity."

▲ In Köprülü Kanyon National Park, the river has carved a canyon almost 9 miles (14 km) long. This park lies in the mountains northeast of Antalya.

Focus on: Ecotourism in Çirali

A pilot project led by the WWF in Çirali, on Turkey's southwestern coast, has shown how economic development and conservation of the environment can go hand-in-hand. One specific problem was that construction of tourist facilities was threatening the nesting sites of loggerhead turtles on the beaches. In consultation with local people, buildings that were illegally constructed too close to the beach were removed. The need for local people to make a living was addressed by training some people as nature guides, opening up nature paths, and promoting the area as a center for ecotourism. Education about the loggerhead turtles and monitoring of the beaches has led to an increase in the numbers of turtle nests. The WWF hopes to use the lessons learned from Çirali to start similar projects elsewhere along Turkey's southwestern coast.

CHAPTER 14

Future Challenges

Turkey is a beautiful country that lies in a geographically strategic position between east and west. It has huge potential, but it faces several key challenges at the start of the 21st century.

EU MEMBERSHIP

Turkey's road to membership in the European Union is long and complex. Although accession negotiations formally opened in 2005, they are "an open-ended process, the outcome of which cannot be guaranteed," according to the framework for talks between the two sides. Once such negotiations have started, however, it is unprecedented in EU history for a country not to gain membership eventually, although the process could take up to 10 years. The negotiations require Turkey to adopt EU law and to settle its differences with its neighbors, specifically Greece and Cyprus, before it can become a member. Turkey will need to work hard to convince many of the more skeptical countries that it should be a part of the EU. Although it is not a formal requirement for EU membership, many people also want Turkey to address its past and acknowledge the deaths of the Armenians in 1915 as a genocide. Many Turks, however, are adamant that this is out of the question, and the suggestion that Turkey should acknowledge that it commited genocide on the Armenians is seen in Turkey as a way of deliberately blocking the country from the EU. Nevertheless, there has been increasing discussion in Turkey about what happened to the Armenians in World War I. In 2005, an academic conference was held in Istanbul at which the issue was discussed.

HUMAN RIGHTS

In the past, Turkey's human-rights record has been one of the major areas of concern in EU membership talks. Today, issues such as honor killings and freedom of speech remain high on the agenda, with severe criticism from the EU for the

▶ In October 2005, the Nationalist Movement Party held a rally in Ankara to protest the start of accession talks between Turkey and the EU.

◀ A Kurdish woman holds a portrait of PKK leader Abdullah Ocalan during a demonstration in 2005 in Strasbourg, France. About 10,000 Kurdish protesters demanded the release of Ocalan, who is serving a life sentence in a Turkish prison.

trial of Orhan Pamuk in 2005-2006. In 2005, the European Court of Human Rights upheld Turkey's government's ban on the wearing of the headscarf in workplaces and educational establishments, claiming that the ban was based on principles of equality and secularism. Some Islamic human rights organizations, however, criticized the decision, saying that the ban was excluding thousands of women from education and professional life.

THE KURDS

The situation of the country's Kurdish population is another thorny issue for Turkey's government to resolve. Turkey is increasingly nervous about increased Kurdish political power in neighboring Iraq. At the same time, the end of the PKK's extended cease-fire has seen renewed violence in the southeast of the country between the PKK and government troops. In July 2005, a blast on a tourist bus that killed five people in the resort of Kusadasi, on the country's west coast, was suspected to be the work of the PKK. Such attacks, which target

the tourist industry—one of the most important areas of Turkey's economy—are a serious problem for the country's government.

CYPRUS

Cyprus will be a major stumbling block in EU accession talks unless Turkey and Greece can come to an agreement. After the failure of the UN-backed plan in 2004, the UN has been reluctant to engage in any further negotiations between the two countries. Turkey continues to refuse to recognize the Republic of Cyprus and to allow Greek Cypriot ships and planes to use its ports and airports. These conditions bar Turkey from membership in the EU under custom unions rules.

Despite all these problems, Turkey remains a country with immense potential. It can look to the future with great hope. In the words of Nobel Prize-winning Turkish novelist Orhan Pamuk: "I see Turkey's future as being in Europe, as one of many prosperous, tolerant, democratic countries."

Time Line

c. 20,000 B.C. Nomadic hunter gatherers roam the region.

c. 6000 B.C. Urban settlement of Çatalhöyük.

c. 2000 B.C. Hittites migrate from central Asia.

546 B.C. Persians conquer part of Anatolia.

334 B.C. Greeks under Alexander the Great overthrow Persians.

323 B.C. Death of Alexander; Anatolia fragments into independent states.

133 B.C. Anatolia part of Roman Empire.

A.D. 313 Edict of Milan, granting freedom of worship to Christians in the Roman Empire.

330 Emperor Constantine creates a new imperial capital in the ancient city of Byzantium (Constantinople).

1071 Battle of Manzikert; Seljuk Turks extend their territories across much of Anatolia.

1096 First Crusade starts in Constantinople.

1243 Mongols invade Anatolia and defeat Seljuks.

1301 Osman I, founder of the Ottoman dynasty, defeats a Byzantine army.

1453 Ottomans capture Constantinople (Istanbul).

1520–1566 Rule of Süleyman the Magnificent.

1526 Ottomans defeat Hungarians at Battle of Mohács – and go on to conquer most of Hungary.

1571 Ottoman fleet defeated at Battle of Lepanto.

1774 Treaty of Kuchuk Kainarji allows Russian ships access to Ottoman waters.

1914–1918 World War I; Turkey fights on the side of Germany and Austria-Hungary.

1915 Turkey massacres the Armenians; Ottomans defeat Allies at Gallipoli.

1918 Armistice ends World War I; Istanbul occupied.

1919 Greek forces invade Turkey; Mustafa Kemal launches movement for national liberation.

1920 Ottoman Empire signs Treaty of Sèvres with victorious powers, surrendering large areas of Anatolia; the treaty is rejected by Turkish nationalists.

1922 Greek army defeated by Turkish nationalists in War of Independence.

1923 Treaty of Lausanne; Sultanate abolished; proclamation of the Republic of Turkey.

1925 Start of Mustafa Kemal's modernizing reforms.

1930 Women gain the right to vote in Turkey.

1934 Turkish Grand National gives Mustafa Kemal the name "Atatürk," or "father of the Turks."

1938 Death of Mustafa Kemal Atatürk.

1939 Earthquake in Erzincan kills more than 30,000.

1939–1945 World War II; Turkey neutral until 1945.

1945 Turkey helps to found the United Nations.

1946 Start of multiparty democracy.

1952 Turkey becomes part of NATO.

1960 First military coup in Turkey.

1960s Tension between Turkey and Greece over Cyprus;

1971 Second military coup.

1974 Turkey invades Cyprus to protect Turkish Cypriots; partition of Cyprus begins.

1978 Founding of Kurdistan Workers' Party (PKK).

1980 Third military coup.

1980s Campaign of terrorism by PKK begins.

1983 Civilian government re-established.

1995 Islamist Welfare Party comes to power in coalition.

1998 Constitutional Court bans Welfare Party.

1999 Izmit earthquake; Abdullah Ocalan captured; Turkey becomes a candidate for EU membership.

2000 PKK announces cease-fire.

2002 AKP has outright victory in elections; Turkey abolishes death penalty.

2004 PKK ends cease-fire; UN-backed plan to create a United Cyprus Republic fails.

2005 EU membership talks begin.

2006 Court case against novelist Orhan Pamuk collapses; Pamuk is awarded the Nobel Prize for Literature; Pope Benedict XVI makes a controversial visit to Turkey.

2007 Hrant Dink, a prominent Turkish-Armenian editor, is murdered in Istanbul.

Glossary

accession becoming part of an organization or accepting a treaty

activist someone who takes direct action to promote a particular political or social point of view

Alevis Muslims who belong to the Shi'a branch of Islam, although their beliefs include elements from many other sources

Anatolia the Asian part of Turkey

archaeological having to do with the study of the remains of ancient civilizations

biomass fuels fuels that are produced from organic matter

caravanserai a kind of inn that provided shelter and hospitality for caravans across the trade routes of Asia

coalition an alliance between two or more political parties in a parliamentary democracy in order to form a government

Cold War the conflict between the United States and the Soviet Union that began after World War II, during which the two counties competed to spread their political systems and to influence other countries but did not fight each other directly

constitution a set of rules governing a country or organization

Crusades the wars fought by Christian powers during the 11th, 12th, and 13th centuries in order to win the Holy Land from the Muslims

cuneiform a type of ancient writing using wedge-shaped characters

deforestation the clearance of trees from land that was once covered by forest

delta the mouth of a river where the river splits into many small tributaries

democracy a political system in which representatives are chosen by the people in free elections

desertification the process by which fertile land becomes barren desert

dynasty a series of rulers from the same family who succeed one another

ecotourism tourism that is designed to help local environments and people and not damage them

epicenter the point on the surface of the earth directly above the center of an earthquake

ethnic having to with a group of people who have shared customs, beliefs, and, often, language

fez a red felt hat without a brim, and often topped with a tassel

genocide the deliberate mass killing of a particular national or ethnic group

human rights the basic rights possessed by all people, including liberty and justice

hydroelectric power (HEP) electricity produced by the harnessing of the power of moving water

inflation the increase, over time, in the price of goods

infrastructure the facilities needed for a country to function, such as communications systems, utilities, and roads

Islamist having to do with a movement that emphasizes Islamic values and traditions and sees Islam as a political system as well as a religion

liberal having to do with someone who favors individual freedom, as well as progress and reform

literacy the ability to read and write

malaria a tropical disease transmitted through the bites of infected mosquitoes

Middle East the region of southwest Asia and north Africa that stretches east-to-west from Libya to Afghanistan

minerals the nonliving substances of which rocks are made

missionary someone who travels to places to convert people to his or her religion

Mongols nomadic peoples from Central Asia who united under their leader Genghis Khan in 1206 and established an empire across most of Asia

mosque a place of worship for Muslims

municipal having to do with a local government

nationalist someone who has great loyalty and devotion to his or her own country and, often, seeks to promote its interests

nomadic having to do with people who move from place to place, often to look for fresh grazing for their herds of animals

nutrients substances used by living beings as food

penal code the laws that relate to crime and punishment

peninsula a strip of land that projects from a larger area of land into water

phytoplankton microscopic plants that live in the oceans and seas

plateau an area of high, flat ground

recession a time of diminished in economic activity

referendum a national vote on a particular issue

republic a country with an elected, rather than hereditary, head of state

sanitation the systems, including sewers, provided to carry away waste

secular not religious

Shi'a Muslims who believe that religious authority can lie only with direct descendants of the Prophet Muhammad

smog thick air pollution

Soviet Union a communist country that existed from 1917 to 1991 that was made up of 15 republics, including Russia

squatter someone who occupies land illegally

Sufi having to do with the mystical beliefs of Islam

sultan the ruler of a Muslim country

Sunni the branch of Islam made up of Muslims who believe that religious authority lies with the person best able to uphold the customs and traditions of Islam

tectonic having to do with the study of the movement of the plates that make up Earth's crust

urbanization the movement of people from rural areas to towns and cities

Further Information

BOOKS TO READ

Barber, Nicola. *Istanbul* (Great Cities of the World). World Almanac Library, 2006.

Bodnarchuk, Kari. *Kurdistan: Region Under Siege* (World in Conflict). Lerner Publishing Group, 2000.

Harmon, Daniel E. *Turkey* (Modern Middle East Nations and Their Strategic Place in the World). Mason Crest Publishers, 2003.

Kemal, Neriman. *Turkey* (Countries of the World). Gareth Stevens, 2001.

Kherdian, David. *The Road from Home: The Story of an Armenian Girl.* Sagebrush, 1999.

Lace, William W. *The Unholy Crusade: The Ransacking of Medieval Constantinople* (Lucent Library of Historical Eras). Lucent Books, 2006.

Lashnits, Tom. *Recep Tayyip Erdogan* (Major World Leaders). Chelsea House Publications, 2005.

Orr, Tamra. *Turkey* (Enchantment of the World, Second Series). Children's Press, 2003.

Pavlovic, Zoran. *Turkey* (Modern World Nations). Chelsea House Publications, 2004.

Sheehan, Sean. *Turkey* (Cultures of the World). Benchmark Books, 2004.

USEFUL WEB SITES

BBC Country Profiles: Turkey
news.bbc.co.uk/1/hi/world/europe/country_profiles/1022222.stm

CIA World Factbook: Turkey
www.cia.gov/cia/publications/factbook/geos/tu.html

Ministry of Culture and Tourism
www.kultur.gov.tr/EN/

New York Times: Turkey
topics.nytimes.com/top/news/international/countriesandterritories/turkey/index.html?inline=nyt-geo

Turkish Embassy in Washington, D. C.
www.turkishembassy.org/index.php

Publisher's note to educators and parents: Our editors have carefully reviewed these Web sites to ensure that they are suitable for children. Many Web sites change frequently, however, and we cannot guarantee that a site's future contents will continue to meet our high standards of quality and educational value. Be advised that children should be closely supervised whenever they access the Internet.

Index

Page numbers in **bold** indicate pictures.

About the Author

Anita Ganeri is a highly experienced author of children's informational books, specializing in geography and religion. She has traveled widely throughout Europe and Asia.